The Quiet

The Quiet

Poems of Endurance

Jonathan E. Wilson

RESOURCE *Publications* • Eugene, Oregon

THE QUIET
Poems of Endurance

Resource Publications
An Imprint of Wipf and Stock Publishers
199 W. 8th Ave., Suite 3
Eugene, OR 97401

www.wipfandstock.com

PAPERBACK ISBN: 979-8-3852-7556-4
HARDCOVER ISBN: 979-8-3852-7557-1
EBOOK ISBN: 979-8-3852-7558-8

VERSION NUMBER 04/03/26

Dedicated to:

My son David Keita Wilson.

My father Jerry Mathern.

Words strain,
Crack and sometimes break, under the burden,
Under the tension, slip, slide, perish,
Decay with imprecision, will not stay in place,
Will not stay still.

—T.S. Eliot, “Burnt Norton”

Contents

Prologue

These poems were written during a year I will never forget. On February 13, 2025, my son was diagnosed with a brain tumor. He underwent his first surgery on March 18 and a second surgery on May 22. In late September, I received word that my father was in critical condition in Oregon. I flew from Tokyo to be with him, and he died on October 6.

I wrote these poems in real time—not as reflections on crisis, but as dispatches from inside it. They are in conversation with poets who have walked before me: Joseph Addison, Emily Jane Brontë, George Gordon Byron, and T.S. Eliot. Their words on hope, solitude, and the pursuit of quiet became my companions when I needed them most.

I am an American living in Tokyo, where I work with children who have experienced trauma from disaster and war. This year, trauma came home. My son is alive. These poems are how I held on.

Acknowledgments

My gratitude to the surgeons and medical staff at Juntendo in Tokyo who

saved my son's life—twice,

To my son, David Keita Wilson,

To my wife, Rie and my son's oyomesan Noel,

To the poets who walked before me and left their words as companions,

And to God who saved us.

PART I FEBRUARY

Hope Renewed—February 17, 2025

I've seen in eyes an empty stare
seeing nothing, tired of searching,
caring for what isn't there
through each day soullessly lurching.
I've watched them hide the pain away.
Retreat from sight, sound, and life,
so in their rooms alone they stay,
cut—quick and deep—a cruel knife.

I've been to places that are no more.
That once were full of noise and bustle,
buying ice cream at the store,
nothing left but stones and rubble.

I've walked along that hopeless street
and sat beside the empty stares,
inviting them outside to meet
others who can share their cares.
Into these places I bring my own
—a store of hope I dip into.

I've learned that when all hope has flown
It still can be—found anew.

In conversation with Emily Jane Brontë's "Hope"

Tokyo Solitude—February 18, 2025

This city is a home for thirty-seven,
a number multiplied a million times.
To get away from all of them is heaven,
to find myself alone is quite sublime;
to slip slow into tub after a climb,
the water's warmth on weary skin to feel,
ripples repeating as in quiet rhyme,
head bowed, eyes closed, so none this peace can steal
—my solitude—in crowded bathhouse real.

In conversation with George Gordon Byron's "There Is Pleasure in the Pathless Woods"

Hope—February 20, 2025

As I along the misty stream in hope
of finding beauty that would help me cope
with news so bad I fell into dismay
unnerved by what the doctors had to say
for on the chart they pointed to a cloud
that hung over my thoughts—Oh dreary shroud!
Now last night's rain has loosened up the soil,
so river's glass shows only my turmoil.
On fairer days that water always shone
with true reflection of pure heaven-tone
for I would stroll amidst this scene I love
and find my heart drawn up to sky above.
That such a stream I once again could see
—hues from on high, not just reflecting me.

In conversation with Joseph Addison's "Hope"

PART II MARCH

Vocabulary—March 8, 2025

As a child I read
voraciously,
anything
I could get my hands on;
library books, encyclopedias,
Reader's Digest's
"How to Increase Your Word Power."

As a teen I pored
over roots from Latin and Greek
seeking to beat
the SAT and score
an entrance to
institutions elite;
a source of power.

As of now
I no longer want
to have to learn new words,
"sphenoid meningioma"
holds no fascination
only reminding me of—that—over
which I have no power.

Complete—March 9, 2025

Son questioning
sacrificial offering without a lamb,
obedient march to Moriah
father lifted his eyes on the third day and saw.

Thrown into the sea,
sacrifice to calm its raging storm,
cast out of God's sight,
yet after three days vomited onto dry land.

Mocked, scourged, crucified,
in my place He died, the sacrifice
that on the third day
makes reconciliation complete.

Freedom—March 14, 2025

Michelangelo's marble
contained angels yearning for
freedom from stone entombment.

What if forms of verse have such
beings trapped within their lines;
literary release for
individualistic
spirits anticipating
the culmination when each
one of us set free—believes

with those emancipated,
carved out of rock—word composed
—rewombed invigorated
all finally perfected?

PART III APRIL

Between—April 18, 2025

A certain state,
after announcements,
before beginnings,
when plans have been made,
but nothing has quite started.
A time of anxious waiting,

hating every minute of life in limbo.
Yet, in a state of shock
after the doc's announcement,
beginning to have feelings of dread
without plan, without warning,
everything starting at once.
No time to wait,
hating every second of life akimbo.

In between, a statement
announced, proclaimed,
a new beginning,
planned, beforehand,
started when the world began.
Waited for with anticipation
of life anew—He is risen!

Picking—April 25, 2025

“Strawberry Picking”
read the hand-written sign
along the highway instigating
a smart U-turn—to check it out.
Nobody there, your quick
phone call confirmed
they were done picking for the day,
but on the way out . . .
“Since you are here,
Go on in.” The greenhouse—
rows and rows of ripening fruit.
We lucked out.
Condensed milk—
for dipping—
sweetness added to sweet berries,
but it’s your smile I cannot live without.

Describing Poetry—April 29, 2025

Eliot's escape
Frost's finding
Wordsworth's tranquility
Poe's rhythmical creation
Levertov's practice of attention
Thomas' contribution to reality
St. Vincent Millay's valuable mistakes
Auden's expression of mixed feelings
Collin's reassembling of what has been scattered
Shakespeare's giving airy nothing a local habitation and a name
I write because before I do my thoughts are anonymous hobos
wandering shepherdless bleating sheep
lost, confused, individual voices
false starts, yet starts the same
making the meaningless mean
focusing past distraction
composing tempos
relaxing restraints
discovering
liberation

Most Powerful Drug—April 29, 2025

A jolt of lightning to the brain,
or liquid calm poured through your veins—
a one-way pass to altered states,
erasing pain, you're feeling great.
This uber drug can do it all:
taking you high, making you fall;
on trips that will expand your mind,
or let you leave your hurts behind.
I'll let you dip in my supply,
a fix so good you cannot buy—
unless you choose the full immerse
into this hit of rhyme and verse.
But if you do, I can predict:
you soon will be a poem addict.

"Words are, of course, the most powerful drug used by mankind."
—Rudyard Kipling

PART IV MAY

Vision—May 6, 2025

Weight presses,
seeking release,
driving forward
though impossibility
shadows. Shadows,
not pitch
suggesting faint
horizon line
awaiting dawn.

Dove of Peace—May 24, 2025

Heavy,
unbidden out-breaths
betray tortuous contortions unseen,
worry-thought burdened brows that
desperately need dove supplied
knowledge-surpassing peace.

PART V JUNE

The Quiet—June 5, 2025

I.

I feel that feeling that never
stays completely submerged
but haunts the undergrowth of memories.
Nothing particular, stalking today's particulars,
always ready to burst from the depths,
bleakening what should be perfectly acceptable.
Tasks to be done. People to meet.
Conversations about ordinary things become unbearable.
I take a walk.

As footfall follows footfall, footfalls
find their way to the shady forest trail.
Branches pierced by dappled spears of light,
none reaching far to pierce the gloom
surrounding primordial ferns, curling fronds like hands
clutching to hold something—something
that should have been released long ago.
Perhaps there is nothing left, an ancient memory
dissolved ages ago, leaving behind
only an instinctive impulse
to hold on.

Holding on to handholds I climb
up through the canyon, walls towering
above, erasing any errant ray of light.
Yet there is reason to praise shadows.
Shadows formed by massive rock
blocking out the all-too-bright clarity of day.
The heat—oppressing, harsh and unrelenting—
could not find the fragile lilies about to open,
blooms that soon would decorate the forest floor,
waiting for their time that was not yet,
was not yet ripe, needing a few more days
of shady quiet.

I stop and rest, leaning back,
feeling the mossy wall's coolness, damp
through my sweat-stained shirt.
Seeing wisps of cloud, rising mist—
not from storm but from me, face flushed
from exertion, releasing extra heat
into the shadow's soft embrace.
Sinking down to sit upon some stone
once positioned at higher elevation
but tumbled down—down into darkness,
down into the shady quiet.
Interrupted only by the persistent
buzzing of a fly attempting to invade
my tempting solitude, propelling me
to hold on once more,
pull myself up,
and continue that walk along the forest trail.

II.

Though the forest might seem still
there's always just behind a tree
some little bird about to trill,
singing lusty for a mate,
a melody for him innate,
or maybe just because he's free
to fly at will into the sky.
There is no need for him to wait
or climb the next branch up the tree—
fly up high enough to see
higher than can you or I,
higher than the fly, he soars,
cascading notes from throat outpours,
falling down to forest floor
where once more for quiet I wait.

In the dark before dawn, or drowsy-hour afternoon, though it's still,
there still is something stirring up the stillness.
A noise.
Though I listen closely as I walk I cannot hear the quiet unless I stop.
The noise is me.
In the dark before dawn, or drowsy-hour afternoon the noise is me.
I'm the one whose footfalls echo,
disturbing peaceful slumberers who once more take flight—
raucous shriek-complaining of my presence in their Eden,
an infidel unobservant of this sacred sanctuary.

But listen closely while I'm still, and forest starts to come alive:
breezes blowing branches together in rhythmic percussion,
a tiny tympani of drops from last night's rain rolling off
leaves above to splash down upon the leaves below.
I don't know which is which, but insects each play their instruments.
All this noise is accompanied by the steady drone of the city—
not far away—humming with the activity of the human hive,
busy about its business, driving cars and buses, building streets
    and houses,
unaware, unconcerned, with this quiet they intrude upon.
This noise that ignores us and ours unless we get too close.

I am too close, so unless I stay still, the forest hides or runs away.
I want to hear their symphony so that other noise is drowned
    out—canceled,
a negative wave to stop the sound
that constantly breaks in, distracting.
But the sound is me. Not just the footfalls crunching on dry leaves—
the sound is in me,
underneath the skin,
the feelings screaming,
instinctual holding,
desperate climbing,
so I have to keep walking.

III.

The brightness of day
as I trudge back through city streets
beats down on rows of commuters

lining up to board buses and trains,
to take us into the warrens of offices
where feelings must remain subterranean.
Shadows are obliterated under fluorescent lights,
illuminating workspaces flickering, screens
collecting every last scrap of data,
storing hoards that never decay, dissolve—
with ever multiplying memory,
so we hold on to everything.

The spotlight shines brightest
at the very top, for those who have reached
the pinnacle of ambition, power, success.
Studied and emulated, analyzed for hints
of weakness to exploit by those
desperately climbing.

The city is dying of noise—
overwhelmed by competing sounds
unable to find a key or rhythm.
The only distinguishable pattern in this mad cacophony
is the ever-increasing tempo.
Overstimulated, we crawl into cubicles,
blocking out everything and everyone only to be trapped
by unrelenting digital demands.
Concentrated on concentration,
but nevertheless distracted.

Nothing left to do but keep climbing,
holding on,
feelings lurking just below the surface.

IV.

In the shadows, something stirs. I look
underneath the forest canopy along a pleasing brook.
I spy a tiny hand, newborn child, but surely not
a human child? As another glance I took
I saw it was a macaque held against its mother's breast.
Still
without a care sustained
I stood silent, entranced.
Nothing intervened, disturbed the quiet of the forest.

V.

The quiet is not the absence of sound, as if
the absence of sound were even possible.
Perhaps in space, but here on earth
there is always noise,
if not from without, then it comes from within.
Quiet is broken, alarms are sounded,
punctuating stillness with active beats
bubbling up from below, percolating through the respite
impossible to maintain. The quiet is ephemeral, lasting
only as long as cherry blossoms in spring.
One moment is blissful serenity only to be caught up
in a blizzard of petals strewn haphazard by an uncaring wind.

Unpredictable, it cannot be scheduled with any real certainty
no more than one could choose what dream will
be shown on tonight's nocturnal theater.
The quiet will come when it comes. Not when we seek it, desire it,
least of all when we are desperate for it.
When we seek it first, it is subtracted,
fleeing from the intrusion.

I find my rest, my solitude, by making it my habit
to put myself in sacred space, in realms where there is shade.
There I find a taste of silence that slides along the tongue eliciting
  a sigh
and occupying the mouth with better things to do than talk.
There I find the fragrance of peace,
a pleasing aroma that calms an anxious soul,
leaving little space for all my protestations to intervene.
There I find I'm safe to feel, protected in the shadow,
held secure without care.

I cannot stay, and sometimes it does not find me,
but I walk along the forest trail, underneath the leafy boughs
hoping that today I will once again meet the Quiet.

In conversation with T.S. Eliot's "Burnt Norton"

PART VI OCTOBER

2025—September 28, 2025

Oyomesan caught herself saying
"¡Ay, ay, ay!"
just learning of his
diagnosis.
"My mother-in-law's word!"

Picked up in the 80's
Santa Barbara, waitressing at a Japanese
restaurant, cooks all Mexican.
"Teriyaki, tempura, miso. Five for here seven to go!"
"¡Ay, ay, ay!"

After each doctor visit
each tense discussion
each seizure, each procedure
each release of halted breath
exhale forgotten.
"¡Ay, ay, ay!"

A word is chosen each year
To best describe, epitomize
its essence.
2025—for us?
¡Ay, ay, ay!

Model 'A' Ford—October 3, 2025

Gently handed
small model
shaky hands once strong
enough to manhandle engine mounts
Asked what it was—"Dunno"

Every part number
known by heart
Taken apart,
pieced together,
fiddled incessantly
Until ignition start and hum

Hands stained like oil
incessantly fiddle
Invisible pieces
assemble, disassemble
"What you working on?"
'Carburetor'
beautiful word.

Went in
simple repair
Came back
Everything out of alignment
Fluids leaking

“How many of your friends
Have this car?”
Asking again
Assembling
“S’pose they all do.”
Piecing it together

PART VII NOVEMBER

Water Always Wins—November 14, 2025

Crashing surf, steady drips,
moisture seeping, storm surge raging—
matters little
what form it's in.
Water always wins.

Waves beat stony shore
until it fits inside an hourglass.
Mountains erode,
iron corrodes—
nothing hard can stay.

And though I dam the flood
lest His precious bottle overflow,
and though I plead for some relief
from drought when there should be
downpours—

There is no dance
to make it start,
no chant, no chart,
no magic medicine
to bring it to an end.

The flow begins and takes away—
salt stinging, current bringing
me along. Who knows
what shape you'll find me in?
Water always wins.

Notes

On Form: The Sudoku Sonnet

For "Freedom," I chose the number seven for a Sudoku Sonnet, a form I played with the year before. The poem has 14 lines broken into three stanzas: a three-line opening, a seven-line middle, and a four-line closing. Each line contains seven syllables, and the middle stanza's lines contain 7, 5, 3, 1, 2, 4, and 6 words respectively. For this poem I felt I needed constraint in the midst of all that was happening.

Poems in Conversation

Several poems in this collection were written in dialogue with earlier poets:

> "Hope Renewed" is in conversation with Emily Jane Brontë's poem "Hope"
>
> "Tokyo Solitude" is in conversation with George Gordon Byron's "There is Pleasure in the Pathless Woods"
>
> "Hope" is in conversation with Joseph Addison's poem "Hope"
>
> "The Quiet" is in conversation with T.S. Eliot's "Burnt Norton," the first of the Four Quartets

About the Author

Jonathan E. Wilson Ph.D. is an American living in Tokyo, Japan pastoring and working globally with children affected by trauma from disaster or war.

www.ingramcontent.com/pod-product-compliance
Lightning Source LLC
LaVergne TN
LVHW020312110826
845148LV00017BA/2638

* 9 7 9 8 3 8 5 2 7 5 5 6 4 *